Your happiness matters

You deserve to be happy.
That little voice in your head
telling you otherwise is fear.
Fear has no concept of the truth.
The truth is happiness wants
YOU – in all your flawed,
imperfect glory.

By Amanda Brewer

This book is dedicated to anyone who has ever been made to feel selfish for wanting to be happy.

To my children, Karlye, Shane, and Nicholas. Thank you for all the moments that cannot be captured with words. Moments of sheer joy, fascination, love, surprise, and faith.

To Chloe and Cooper, thank you for allowing me the opportunity to be whatever you may want me to be in your lives.

To my soulmate Joshua, everything in my life has led me to you. My choices, my heartbreaks, my regrets. When I met you, my past seemed worth it, because if I had done anything differently, I might have never met you. Thank you for always reaching for my hand, thank you for being my home, thank you for supporting me, thank you for fulfilling me, thank you for loving me. Thank you for being you.

To me. I am proud of you.

What's inside

Let's start a movement

I want to start a movement.
Your happiness matters.

Somewhere along the way, society has picked up this disturbing and damaging belief that wanting to be happy is selfish and arrogant. Society has taught us that what we want most in life is just not important, and we do not deserve that.

Society has managed to twist us so far out of alignment with who we really are that we believe that suffering is to be expected and hell, even victorious. So, we have given up on the belief that our happiness matters and that we are just set to live a life of misery because…what would people think?

I am tired of it.
Screw what society thinks about your happiness.

I am here to tell you.
Your happiness matters.
You can be selfish with it.
Be YOU. Do YOU. For YOU

Will you join me?

Wow, how selfish.

Chapter 1

When my kids were younger, I got up at 5:00 am every day. Some people thought that just meant I was a morning person, and when they said that I just laughed and carried on with the day. Truth is, I was not a morning person, I still am not. I love my sleep. I love my warm bed. I just knew I needed that time to do what I needed to do to keep my day productive and I feel better about myself. I would get up, pop the top on an ice-cold Diet Mt. Dew, get in the shower, do my hair and makeup, get dressed. Then I was ready for whatever mood my children were going to wake up in and anything that they needed, I was already awake and ready.

I still do this now that my children are older. If we have something going on that day, I will get up an hour and half to two hours before everyone else. In case Joshua or my children need something when they get up.

When I was 33, during one of those mornings, I had a thought that changed my whole life, and the course that it took. I remember it was around 5:45 a.m. because I remember looking at the time while getting ready. I was putting mascara on, and I looked at myself in the mirror and it was just one of those weird moments, that maybe you have had before. I didn't just glance at myself. I like, really examined myself.

I was not happy.

My happiness mattered to no one in this house.

I started to cry. I cried hard because instantly, I felt
trapped. I felt like the walls were closing in on me. I
remember sitting down on my bathroom floor and just
sobbing. I sat on my bathroom floor for a while and
cried. I thought about my life, I thought about how
truly unhappy I was in my marriage, how I was not
happy at my job, I loved my children, but I was not a
happy mother. I was letting the unhappiness of my
marriage, bleed into everything in my life. But what do
you do with that kind of thinking? Like, where do you
go from there? I picked myself, finished getting ready,
and fell right into the routine of the morning.

After performing my morning motherly duties and
routine once the kids were all at school. I headed to
work. I worked at the Highschool in town, in
administration. It was not my dream job, but it allowed
me to be off when my children were off. So, it worked
for me at the time.

Once there, I flipped my visor down and took another
look at myself. Thinking, I wonder if anyone else
knows how unhappy I am? Of course, they didn't. I am
good at making face, I mean hell I was fooling myself
that I was happy.

Showtime, I thought as I opened the door, while telling
myself. You deserve better than this life. This is not as
good as it gets.

Followed up immediately with the guilt of how you can be so selfish. But was it? What about how I feel?

I spent the majority of my life, putting other people's needs and wants above mine. Not speaking up when I should have, agreeing to things I didn't want to agree to, taking on more than I can carry so others have their hands free. And no, this is not woe is me. I did it. I allowed it. It was my job as a wife and mother, right? Put your family and their needs first. Hell, I didn't even make myself a plate or sit down at the table until my family had been served. But this is the way it's supposed to be. I will find myself once my children are grown and out of the house, right? Isn't that what we tell ourselves when our children are little? How unhealthy is that? Why can't we have it all? Why does society make us feel guilty for wanting to be a lady first, and wife / mom second?

Because duh, that is selfish.

Congrats, you just made it through

the first chapter of this book, I know, it was short. The whole book is short. The following story I want to share with you, it's basically how I discovered that my happiness matters, and how I took back ownership of it…I always had it in me, I just lost it when I lost myself. What worked for me, isn't from a big fancy program, there wasn't a self-help book I read, there wasn't a magical pill or therapy session that I took. It was just me against what society crams down our throat on what is acceptable and what isn't. By announcing that my happiness matters and by taking it back, I lost things. I lost a marriage, I lost friendships, I lost relationships with family.

By my choice and it felt fucking fantastic!

My hope is the book will help you, it will empower you, it will make you realize those thoughts you are thinking…honey they aren't crazy.

You deserve to be happy.

Your happiness matters.

Always keep a piece of you for you.
That is not selfish,
That's survival

Selfish is not black and white.

Chapter 2

For weeks I silently thought about that word.

Selfish.

I mean, I couldn't talk to my girlfriends about how I was feeling. I mean, they would think less of me, right? My marriage was basically done, so I damn sure wasn't talking to him about it.

The webster dictionary defines the word selfish as, (of a person, action, or motive) lacking the consideration for others; concerned chiefly with one's own personal profit or pleasure.

When the word, "selfish" comes to mind, it often sparks negative connotations at first. We automatically think this: self-centered, self-serving, self-involved. Like, we are supposed to avoid thinking only about me and my interest, right?

True the word itself is defined as being concerned with only your own personal pleasure and profit, and the lack of considerations for others around you, however, people still think of the word selfish to mean you're simply putting yourself first.

The world isn't black and white, and the word selfish damn sure isn't. When you board an airplane, and the stewardess is going over safety protocol, what do they tell us about the oxygen mask. Put your mask on first before helping others. Would anyone call us selfish for doing that? Nope.

The same should and DOES ring true about your life. It's not self-sustaining to continue any relationship, job, friendship, marriage, especially if one is abusive, if they do not make you happy. If something is affecting your well-being – well it is time to say goodbye.

By allowing people to steal your happiness, where does that lead you? Nowhere.

We are taught that its selfish to put ourselves first, in society that is considered a big no no, that is bad. So, then because we fear being known as the "bad guy" we stay, and we are unhappy.

And again, where does that get you? Yep. Nowhere.

Let me tell you something, or as Joshua, my soulmate often says, focus in on this. Any concept of being a "bad" person, beyond actually being a bad person, you know like theft or killing someone, is just a mechanism of society to keep you in place. People will talk about how they have made a commitment, and then there are people that say, you will never be happy in your relationship all the time, it'll pass. And then the best one of all, but what about the kids?

All of this is just society keeping you in place.

Sometimes we start down a path without really considering where the path is going. Maybe we never saw the hurdles to the path we started on or maybe the end goal wasn't as clear.

Does not mean that we are selfish.

It means that relationships, tend to just run their courses sometimes. It means sometimes you just got involved into something prematurely and now that you know that your goals have changed. You have changed, and you do not want to spend the rest of your life living in regret and unhappy.

Why is that selfish? Wouldn't it be considered more selfish to stay with someone you do not love? To stay at a job, you aren't getting anything out of just to appease your coworkers or boss? Isn't it more selfish on your children if you are just going through the motions and routines of life just so they can say their parents never divorced? That is selfish to me, that is causing harm. And the person who loses the most in all of those situations is you.

It's not selfish to love yourself, take care of yourself,
and to make your happiness a priority.
It's necessary.
-    Mandy Hale

Walking before running

running

Chapter 3

What do you want to be when you grow up?

Think about many times we are asked this and ask this of our children in a lifetime. I feel like we focus on this for many reasons, but the main one, at least for me, is for direction. We all need to be going in a direction while growing up, a goal. A purpose.

Mine was a wanted to be a wife and a mom. I never faltered from that. I was dead set on becoming a wife and a mom. Looking back, I know it was because I desperately wanted family, and I wanted to be the best wife and mother that ever existed. I had no idea what that truly meant, and I had romanticized it into something that was not healthy for myself.

I was raised by the strongest, smartest, prettiest, most lady like southern lady you ever had the honor of knowing. My grandmother. She was single. Her and my grandpa divorced before I was born, however they remained the best of friends and always had Sunday dinner together. My grandmother told me that they were just better off friends than husband and wife. I never knew them married but seeing them together was something. My grandpa just adored her, and they had playful banter and I just loved being with them. However, looking back, it was a blessing and a curse. Because you see, I grew up thinking that is what divorce looked like.
Boy was I wrong.

In the 3rd grade, I got mono. And since I was not kissing on boys, the only place we can think I got it was from the water fountain. I was in the hospital and ended up missing 3 months of school. The decision was made for me to repeat the 3rd grade because I missed the entire section of multiplication and division and they did not want to send me on that far behind.

My second year of 3rd grade was really my favorite year of school. My teacher was Mrs. Parr, and she was the ultimate lady. I loved the way she dressed. I loved the way she walked. I loved the way she talked. I was just in awe of her, and she was so sweet. She made me happy, and I looked forward to seeing her every day. Now, to age myself, back in my day of school outside people were actually welcomed in the schools, we did not have to worry about the issues we have today. So sometimes Mr. Parr, her husband, would come to the school. He wore suits and always had a smile on his face. Often, he would come up and have lunch with her, or just bring her flowers. I remember telling myself that my husband would wear suits and bring me flowers. I only share this story because every young girl has that one person in their life, that is not family, that makes an impact on them and how they want to see themselves when they grow up. To me, Mrs. Parr was a lady I wanted to be like.

My grandmother taught me how to be a lady. How to sit in a dress, how to wear makeup, always have jewelry on, never leave the house not looking your best. Put your makeup on every day, it will make you feel good about yourself. Your job is to take care of the house. Your job is to take care of the kids, and your job is to be the best wife you can be to your husband.

My grandparents raised me by telling me that I should never need a man, I should want one.

There is a difference.

My grandpa taught me how to change a tire, change my oil, jump start a car, how to use tools, what tools were what. Basically, life skills. Again, with the idea that I should not need a man. I should want one.

They were amazing to me; they took me in when they did not have too. They love me fiercely and thank God every day that I had them.

I was 18 when I left my hometown, the only town I had ever known to begin a new life in a new town.

Fast-forward one year. I was in a relationship and about 120 days later, I was married. Go even further, and I am married for 17 years to a not so nice guy who did not know my value, and we have three children, and I was miserable.

I repeat, sometimes we start down a path without really considering where the path is going. Maybe we never saw the hurdles to the path we started on or maybe the end goal wasn't as clear.

I realized I had succumbed to my 3rd grade self's definition of happiness.

I ran before I knew how to walk.

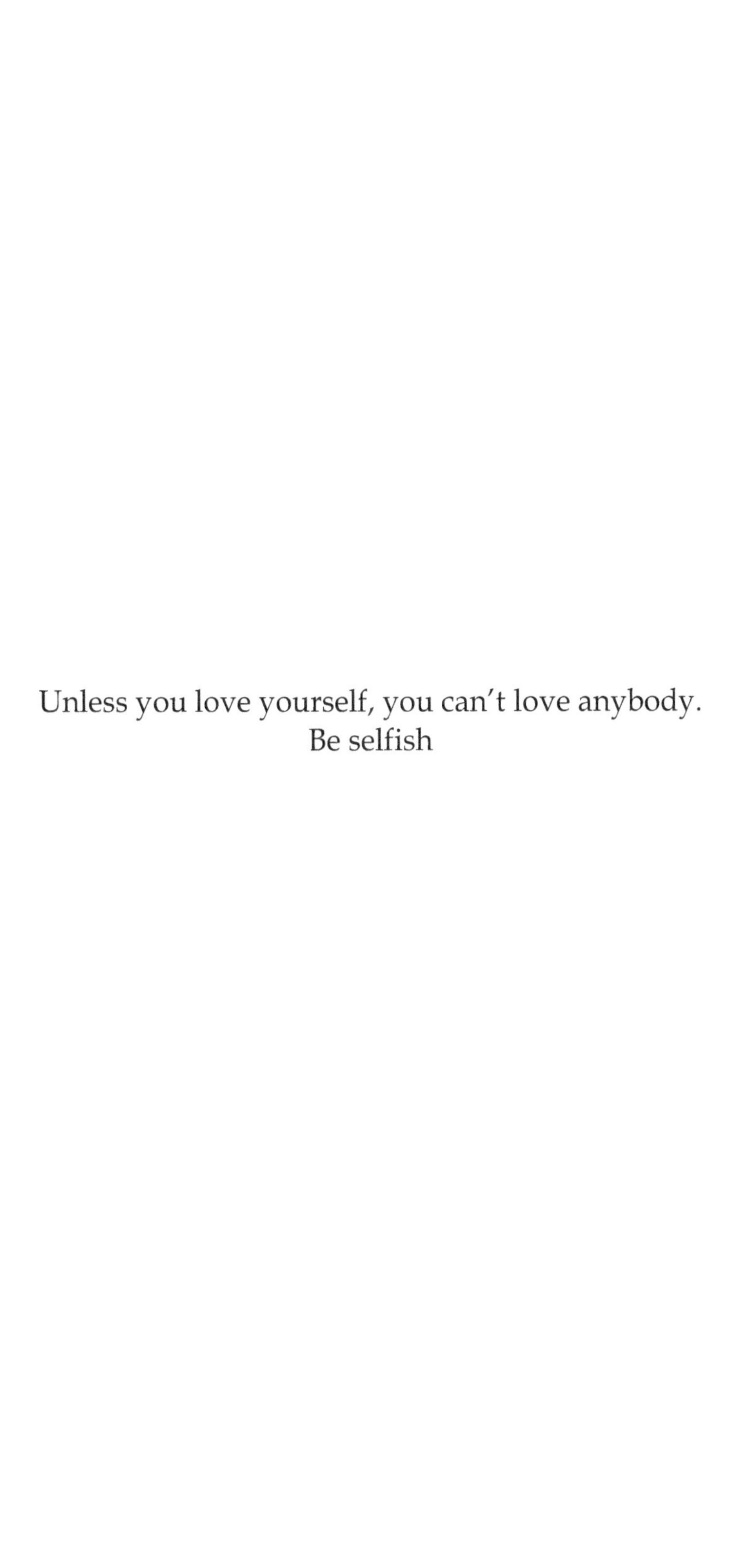

Unless you love yourself, you can't love anybody.
Be selfish

YOLO

Chapter 4

A year before I left my job in the school system, my
boss committed suicide.
I struggled a lot with that. She was the happiest person
I knew, she had a husband, one son, and two dogs that
were her world. How could she of all people take her
life?

After the shock of her actions wore off, I was left again
asking myself where my happiness mattered in my life.
And there were times I thought of her and was jealous
that she got to take the easy way out, and that not only
was I trying to pick up the pieces at work, but I was
also struggling with my personal life.

And it really worried me. If it was not for the strength I
got from my children, I do not know what would have
happened to me. But I knew if I left them, then they
would be with their father, and I was NOT going to do
that to them.

I made the decision that I was getting a divorce.

Many people get into a relationship without asking
themselves a very basic question.

"What do I want from my partner?"

That is not being selfish. If you do not know what kind of person you want, then how in the hell would you know what kind of person is for you?

"What do I need in a partner?"

Do you want to be smothered in love in affection when you're having an off day, or do you want to someone that will give you space? Sounds basic yes. But sadly, it's not that. Because we often do not ask those things, we just go straight into a relationship.

Before we can make a real connection with someone else, we have to be connected with ourselves first.

Your happiness is your responsibility.
Take ownership of it.

YOLO

Okay, I have a little exercise for you.
I need you to grab your phone or laptop and go to YouTube and look up Unbroken by Mateusz M.

During my rough days, I listened to this multiple times a day, in the morning while getting ready, on the way to work, sometimes at work, and then several times in the evening.

Every time I needed some motivation, every time I needed someone to tell me what I was doing was right. I listened to this.

Its 5 minutes and 58 seconds long.
Put the book down, press play, close your eyes, and listen.

Then come back.

.

.

.

.

.

HOW FREAKING COOL WAS THAT!
Are you ready to like run through a wall?
Did you cry?
Did you get goosebumps?

Steve Jobs: *"Your time is limited, so don't waste it living someone else's life. Don't be trapped by dogma – which is living with the results of other people's thinking. Don't let the noise of others opinion drown out your inner voice."*

So many people settle on what they think is right, acceptable, and safe. We then become so dominated by the idea of staying because well, it's scary to move. We sacrifice our own happiness, and we choose to compromise it all because we stay in whatever situation is robbing us of our happiness.

If you are unhappy in your job, quit.

If you are unhappy with the people you surround yourself with, leave.

If you are unhappy with your love life, end it.

If you are unhappy with your city, move.

If you are unhappy with your life path, take any turn possible.

If you are unhappy with how you see life, move your sight.

If you are truly unhappy where you are right now, THEN MOVE.

It is a simple as that. I am tired of people making it so complicated. I was that person. I was the one that got so compliant in my life and the choices I made, I lost myself.

ENOUGH IS ENOUGH!

This should be the ONE thing that is passed on to everyone reading this book.

If you are truly 110% unhappy with where you are right now….

THEN MOVE!

Stop feeling sorry for yourself.
Stop whining.
Stop crying.
Stop bitching.
Stop complaining.
Stop comparing.
Stop dreaming of what it would be like.

It can be all of that and more, if you move your ass!

As you can read, I have passion behind this, because I wish someone would have lit a fire under my ass about this. I wish someone would have looked me in the eyes and said MOVE AMANDA!

I want to light a fire under your ass.
I want you to move IF that is what you truly want.

Les Brown: *"That you going to have some ups and you're going to have some downs. Most people give up on themselves easily. You know that a human spirit is powerful? There is nothing as powerful – it's hard to kill the human spirit! Anybody can feel good when they have their health, their bills are paid, they have happy relationships. Anybody can be positive then. Anybody can have a larger vision then. Anybody can have a lot of faith under those kinds of circumstances. The real challenge of growth, mentally, emotionally and spiritually comes when you get knocked down. It takes courage to act!*
Part of being hungry when you've been defeated.

It takes courage….
To start over again."

Nothing is easy. If it was, well you would have never picked up this book.

You have one chance. I worked every single day for two years with someone I considered a friend. She was only 53 years old when she took the shortcut home. Her death shook me to the core, and really fueled me to not go down the path she did. To not take the shortcut.

This is my life.
This is my only life.

I moved.

Once you learn to be happy,
You won't tolerate being around
People who make you feel
anything less
-     Lela Grace

Redefining Selfishness

Chapter 5

Just because someone defines something you have done as selfish; does not mean you have to define it in their terms.

Your happy ending is not someone else.

It's you.

Your story starts with you.

Do not let the world rob you of all that you could be. Beginning with yourself is always the right way to go.

I read a quote once by Greg Gumucio that said, "I want you to be really, really selfish. The more selfish and nurturing you can be for yourself, the by-product for those that you love or work that you do is greatly enhanced."

After years of trying to be someone I wasn't, doing things I did not want to do, and putting others needs before my own. I decided that I had had enough.

Who am I? I had gone missing, and I wanted to find out where I had gone and bring myself back again.

I got a divorce.
I took my children and I moved away.

I started standing up for myself. If something did not feel right, I gave myself permission to not do it. I gave myself permission, (no matter how uncomfortable it was), to speak up. I gave myself permission to attend my own needs before I attended to anyone else's – knowing that I wasn't doing anyone any good if I was completely lost or resentful or withdrawn because I had pushed myself aside.

At first it was hard. I was so uncomfortable. In all honesty, it was probably my worst fear. Standing up for myself. My whole life, I wanted to be "liked". It was hard. I felt like I was letting people down, I felt like a bad mom. But my soul kept at it, something kept telling me to just stick to being selfish and that your happiness matters! All these feelings I was feeling were just growing / expansion pains that would help me and everyone around me.

We are taught that being selfish is a bad thing. But how can feeling good be bad? How can filling our own cup so we have more to give….be bad? How can loving ourselves be bad?

It is time to redefine the word selfish.

Selfish is simply another way we can do self – care and self – love.

By strengthening the relationship, we have with ourselves we can choose to say YES to you. Remember that being selfish with yourself is not at the expense of others.

We have disowned selfish, deeming it to be bad and wrong. When you say you cannot embrace your selfishness, but what you are really saying is that you cannot even bring yourself into the equation to have your needs met.

To redefine selfish begins with you telling yourself you are worthy of receiving. You are worth of being happy. I bet a lot of you are thinking, but I am in a relationship, I have children, I could do all of this if I was single. But not now.

Wrong. If that was truly the case, then answer me this. How did you get to where you are right now if you have already mastered being selfish with your happiness? If that was the case, when you got into the relationship you would have known to make yourself a priority and not abandoned yourself for the sake of another person.

You are less likely to lose yourself in any relationship if you truly honor yourself and your happiness, and from there you can allow the relationship to honor your happiness.

You will never live a full happy life if you do not rock the boat. You need to listen to those inner whispers that are most likely wails at this point. Everything that you are seeking on the outside needs to be dealt with on the inside first. When you don't take care of yourself, you are going to become resentful.

I believe we are all in one long term relationship and that there is a revolving door. It is our parents, bosses, lovers, siblings, children, friends, and all the other people who will activate us so we can learn what we came here to learn.

I lost myself in my marriage and motherhood, it was a very long time to be missing. Now I have learned that being selfish is actually a good thing and this part of my life is the most I am grateful for, because I found myself. Now that I am no longer trying to be seen in a certain light, or abandon myself to be loved, liked, or accepted – it doesn't bother me as much if I rub someone the wrong way as long as I am staying true to myself and I am doing it with honor and grace. The only thing, and the most important thing, is that I am staying true to me. That is how I have redefined selfish.

Never apologize for leaving a situation
To make yourself happier.
Your health matters and your
Happiness is important

<u>Dog Eat Dog</u>

Chapter 6

I firmly believe that we live in an infinitely abundant world. By taking care of myself, aka being selfish, in no ways takes away from anyone else. It actually gives to them through modeling self-care and also through having more energy for them.

I feel like I need to say that obviously the type of selfishness I am writing about is the one that comes from a place of love. Love for myself and my wellbeing. It is not about wanting to hurt anyone. It is about taking care of ourselves. It is knowing that we matter and are worthy of our own care. It is about telling yourself that it is okay to stand up for yourself and giving yourself permission to not push your own needs to the side or saying yes when we mean no – out of fear that someone might be mad at you.

If you were raised like me, and I am guessing since you made it this far, you were. We were taught to give our shirt off our back if someone needed it. But sometimes, you just have to tell that person no. Or as Chandler from Friends said, "No you cannot have my coat because then I will be cold, if you wanted a coat, you should have brought your own!" ha-ha who remembers that episode?

There are plenty of people who have zero issues leveraging selflessness into their own benefit and will push and push until you break and then cast you away. This isn't to say the world is full of narcissists and sociopaths out to get you, just that they exist, and they will take and take and take from you as long as you allow it. There is nothing wrong with telling someone no if you will not get anything out of it.

"You cannot help others if you cannot help yourself" Very cliché I know, but it gets the point across, right? If you can't even help yourself, how are you supposed to help people around you? If you want to help build houses for the poor, but never even used a hammer before, you aren't going to get much done if you don't take the time to learn how to use the hammer first.

If you want to help others, then get your foundation solid first.

I am not saying it is a dog-eat-dog kind of world and you should just abandon the whole concept of being selflessness, but instead, just take some time to indulge yourself. Say no when you want to, be selfish with your own happiness.

Do not waste your efforts feeding toxic black holes when you could spend the same effort on yourself or people who actually appreciate it. Abandon the concept of being selfish as being a negative. Take time to improve you. You can't save the world if you cannot even safe yourself from your own.

I am willing to bet that if I asked you what kind of person you would want to be, you would say, you want to make an impact on the lives of others. But how can you do that if you are cannot make an impact on your own first?

"I hated every minute of training, but I said, don't quit. Suffer now and live the rest of your life as a champion"
Muhammad Ali

The term neuroplasticity comes to mind. Without analyzing the science of it, the proof of neuroplasticity means that all those motivational quotes you have read have an element of truth behind them. You possess the power to change your lie because you possess the power to rewire your brain.

This is something you have to make a choice at. In order to really earn the right to say my happiness matters, you have to choose it. You have to choose that your happiness matters. Every single person on this earth has that choice.

I want this to become more than a self-help book. All self-help books do is tell you that the journey is tough, you can do it, blah blah blah…

I want you to be motivated.
I want you to dig deep for the motivation to make this long term, I want you to have the courage to put yourself first. Screw that, there is no courage.

I want you to fucking move.

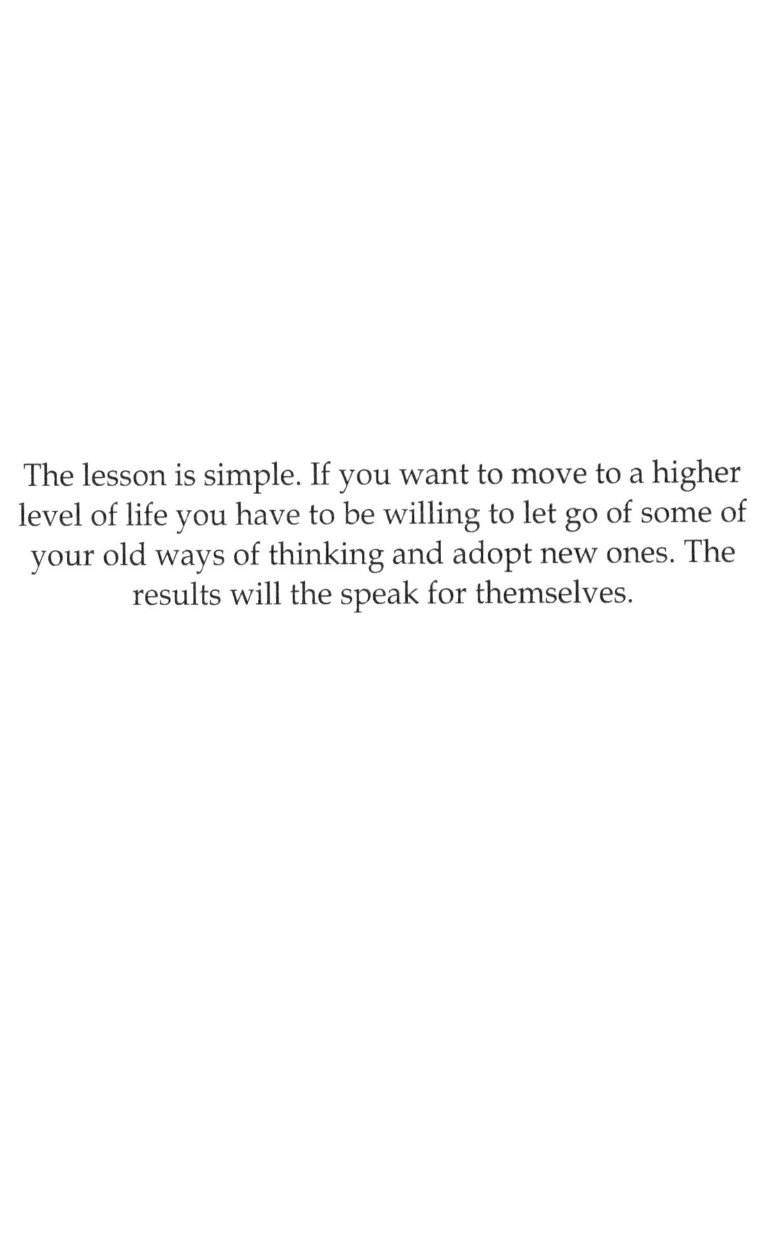

The lesson is simple. If you want to move to a higher level of life you have to be willing to let go of some of your old ways of thinking and adopt new ones. The results will the speak for themselves.

Bullsh*t

Chapter 7

We do not learn by our senses.
We learn by osmosis.

When a mama cow has a calf. She doesn't sit her calf down and have a big discussion on the ways to eat grass. The calf simple sees the momma cow eating and takes note of it.

I will be the first to admit I stayed I my marriage a lot longer than I should have for my children. I think it's pretty normal to want to hang on after you have built a home and life together. No one wants to go at it alone, parent solo, or spend a holiday without your children.

It is easy to tell yourself it's not that bad. And it is REALLY easy to look at your children at the dinner table and tell yourself that you will stay together to save them.

I am speaking from personal experience when I say the following; if you are staying in a relationship that you are not happy in because of your children.

YOU ARE
SELFISH

And not the good selfish.
The bad selfish.

Staying in a marriage where there is no love is not saving your children. Not one little bit.

Sure, it's going to disrupt them, it may hurt them, and that feels unnatural.

Then there is the talk of those around you, "what about the kids?" That is really easy for people who have never experience divorce and then that leaves you second guessing your choice.

Everyone is forgetting the most important part here, the kids.

In my experience, I was teaching my daughter how a man should treat his wife. I was teaching my sons this is how you treat your wife.

How in the hell is that being a good mom?

And guess what else? Your kids know. You're not that slick, they know. Your kids sense the tension, they see the heartache even if they never talk to you about it. When they feel those feelings, it affects them. I don't care how adjusted or communicative they are.

Once I realized that my marriage was not about my children, but about my partnership between me and my ex-husband, I was able to get really clear about divorce and I never experienced any guilt.

Of course, there is an impact on children in divorce, I am not saying otherwise. What I am saying is that if we had stayed married and they found out my miserableness was for their sake…well that would have caused a lot more damage than my divorce ever did.

It takes time, but the kids will adjust to a new life. They adjust to seeing their parents happier for not being together. They get to meet the REAL you.

Children will never adjust to watching the two adults in the house walk around angry and unhappy all the time.

Staying together for your children is a bullshit reason to stay married. Stay together for you separate for you, divorce for you and not for anyone else.

If you are not taking a stand for yourself and your happiness, no one else is going to, regardless of what you sacrifice for them.

Your thoughts matter.
Your problems matter.
Your opinions matter.
Your happiness matters.
Your voice matters.
Your life matters.
You matter.

<u>What makes you…you?</u>

Chapter 8

You get what you settled for. I believe that to be so true. As we age, we are supposed to know ourselves better.

What makes you happy?
What makes you sad?
What excites you?
What terrifies you?

We're supposed to know what to chase so we can go after it.

But many of us, well, we never learn that about ourselves because we did not take the time to be selfish.

I don't believe you need to travel to some long-lost country alone, nor do I believe you need to be some selfish self-absorbed asshole to find out what you want in life. I do believe that everyone needs to take time in our lives to figure out what we want. If it's a house with a picket fence, a big fancy prestigious job with a corner office, if it's a little cottage by the water, if it's to be the next youtuber, or even the President of the United states…. Awesome! But you will never figure that out, if you never put your happiness first.

My grandmother used to tell me you are the only person that can make you happy, and this is 100% true. If you are relying on other people as your source of happiness or even confidence, then it's time to reevaluate what is going on in your life.

By placing yourself first, you will start to learn what inspires you. You will learn what makes you get out of bed in the morning, without anyone telling you too. You will learn what makes you angry, sad, happy, excited. If your thoughts are clouded by other people judgements and opinions – then well how can you ever make a decision for yourself. For yourself.

Putting yourself first does not equal selfish, it equals human being. How can you be independent if you do not focus on yourself? We get one take at life, one. There is no do over, this is it people.

Ever heard "love yourself as much as you want someone else to." How much do you love yourself? How much do you value yourself? Are you a priority in your life?

Demand what you deserve.

Loving yourself does not mean you cannot love others. It means you put value in yourself and then by doing that, you can put value in the people around you.

You. Cannot. Pour. From. An. Empty. Cup

Take ownership of who you are. People will always be prettier, nicer, richer, or have a better life than you. But you are you for a reason. There is literally no one on the planet like you. Sure, there are some that have similar beliefs, values, morals – but honey you are the only you in existence. Stop pretending. Stop faking it. Stop putting on face in spite of the people around you.

"If you want to dress a certain way, live your life a certain way, act a certain way. Then own it. You need to live up to the person you are putting out there. You can do this by accepting who you are." – Lauren Alexander

So who is the best version of yourself?

Perfect happiness can only be achieved if it includes
you.
Therefor it starts with you.
Happy people have a way of making others happy, too.
It has a ripple effect through the whole universe.
Every happy being counts.
The more the better.
Your happiness matters.

Happiness is a civic duty

Chapter 9

Now I feel like I need to roll this back a bit. I want to explain that I am not trying to create a burning of the bra moment. I do not want you to go out and divorce your husband, break it off with your boyfriend, quit your job, or pack up your car and leave.

Well, unless that is going to make you happy, because you deserve that. ☺

There are other ways to put your happiness first and remain at the job you are at or in the relationship you are in. This is just my story. This is what worked for me.

I tried marriage counseling.
I tried personal counseling.
I tried talking.
I tried crying.
I tried and tried and tried…. until I just stopped caring.

I was married for 17 years; the red flags were seen the first week I met the man but being young and dumb…and I repeat starting down a path without really considering where the path is going. The point is, I have no regrets because my children came from that relationship, but it should have never happened.

I am not an expert on relationships, I have no fancy degree in that profession. I am just simply a lady from Oklahoma who went through some stuff and had an itch to tell my story. I want to start a movement; I want to help YOU understand that your happiness matters!

If I can just help one person realize that their happiness matters and that it is okay to be selfish with that – then they will tell someone else, and so on and so on. I want this movement to flood through social media, our lives, our souls.

To all the people who are crying on the bathroom floor at 5:45 a.m. – feeling lost, scared, confused, trapped, and isolated.

I see you.
I hear you.

This is not as good as it gets. I hate that phrase, "well, I guess this is just as good as it gets." BULLSHIT. That is a settler's comment, and honey we are not settlers when it comes to our happiness.

We all get one life. One. There is no do over. We do not make it to the end and Jesus, (or whoever/whatever you see) is there asking if you want to go for another ride. This is it folks.

Society has somehow managed to twist us so out of alignment with WHO WE REALLY ARE that we have come to believe that suffering is expected, hell its even victorious. Someone has told us that and we now believe that if we pursue our own happiness, we will somehow destroy or neglect the happiness of those around us. So that has made us give up on believing that our own happiness matters, and we just resign to settling into a lifetime of misery because God forbid, we might make someone unhappy.

And you know what? That really pisses me off.

Being happy is the single best thing you can do for the ones around you. How many people have you known in your life, that you would describe as a person who "lights up the room" with their presence? How many people have you known that you just loved to be around because they made you feel happy?

Happiness is a ripple effect far beyond just one person. When you are happy, your husband, boyfriend, partner, co-worker, children notice and are influenced by your happiness. That isn't written to just make you feel good, that is backed by science. When you are truly happy, you can boost the mood with anyone you encounter, and here is where it gets really rad…. those people then carry that to someone else, and so on and so on.

Pretty cool right?

And 10000000000000% possible with you!

There was a study done and published in 2008 called the happiness "cascade effect."
Researchers from Harvard and the University of California, San Diego discovered that "clusters of happiness result from the spread of happiness and not just a tendency for people to associate with similar individuals" and that the happiness of single individuals affects even those they do not know…through three degrees of separation!

What does that mean? If you are happy, not only does that make your people happier, but it also makes the people they are around happier, and then the people they are around happier, too!

[I]f one person is happy, that increases the chances of happiness in a friend living within a mile by 25 percent. The "cascade" effect, as researchers put it, continues: a friend of the friend has almost a 10 percent higher likelihood of being happy, and a friend of that friend has a 5.6 percent increased chance.

Happiness is contagious. So, pretty damn far from being considered selfish, do you agree?
Look at it this way, the pursuit of your happiness can be seen as a public service – maybe even considered a civic duty of sorts.

Success is awarded
To those willing
To do the
Uncomfortable
-    Darren Hardy

<u>Comfortably Uncomfortable</u>

Chapter 10

I have a question for you, have you ever driven your car somewhere, a place you go repeatedly, and by the time you reach your destination you barely remember what happened after you got in the car?

Routines have a way of making us feel at ease and in control. But you know what constant routines really do. They dull your senses. Discomfort goes a long way when it comes to self-development.

What is my point?

When you first decide that your happiness matters, you are going to see your life differently. Those rose-colored glasses are going to become clear, and you are going to see what and who is making you unhappy. You are going to change routine. You are going to make some people uncomfortable. Hell, some of the people might see a brand new you, because you have never been one to stand up for yourself before, so what has gotten into to you. You are probably going to hear, "well it never bothered you before" or "why would we change that this is what works" and you are going to have to reply to those statements.

And it's not going to be comfortable at first. You are going to want to just go back to the comfort of that routine, in fact your body is going to crave it. You're going to think, this is just not worth the fight, the drama, the rejection, and you are going to want to quit. To settle.

I am here to tell you, girl this is just where it starts to get fun!

Being uncomfortable is something you should embrace. Putting yourself in new and unfamiliar situations releases dopamine, you know the good stuff that our body produces to MAKE YOU HAPPY! Here is where it gets really wild, that unique part of the brain is only activated when you see or experience something completely new.

The world is geared towards removing obstacles from your life. Remotes change the channels on the television, you can turn the room temperature down from your phone, cars start themselves, hell some even drive themselves, (no thank you!) you can shop from your phone, on your couch and someone then delivers it to your door. While all of this is nice - you got it comfortable, but it can make us lose touch when we are faced with a difficult task, it can appear more daunting and stressful than it truly is, because we have been weaned off of dealing with obstacles.

You deciding to be selfish with your happiness is going to create some obstacles in life. But it's going to be okay, because you are going to prepare for it, you are ready for it, you are okay with being uncomfortable because why? Say it with me….MY HAPPINESS MATTERS DAMN IT!

Staying comfortable is going to get you nowhere, I lie, it's going to get you to the same place you already are. It is inside of being uncomfortable that you grow, you develop confidence, and then self – belief happens.

Do not become wallpaper.
No, that is not a typo. I just wrote do not become wallpaper. Humor me.

You just redid the family room, and you have a beautiful accent wall, and its wallpaper. Its bold and makes a statement when people walk in the room. Every time someone walks in the room, it catches their eyes. They comment on it.

Fast forward 6 months. It is noticed by new people who come over, and when you post on social media someone might comment on it, but the people who see it every day. Well, it's no longer noticeable. Because it has blended in. Fast forward even further, now the sun has probably faded it some, it's been banged on, knocked into, parts are peeling…and its unappealing.

When things are new and fresh, they are exciting. They are discussed, they are shown off. After a while if they are not changed up a little, they start to blend in. That is what we do to ourselves, (see I told you I had a point), by neglecting your happiness, you have become the wallpaper on the wall. No one notices you anymore, and you're just a part of the walls.

Aren't you worth more than to be compared to wallpaper?

Yes, the answer is hell yes, I am!

So, get comfortable being uncomfortable. Wallpaper is a pain the ass to get down and replace. Realizing that your happiness matters is going to feel the same way to in the beginning, but once you peel that wallpaper away you are going to see that beauty that you have been covering up for years, layer by layer it is going to come off the wall. And it is going to be glorious girl!

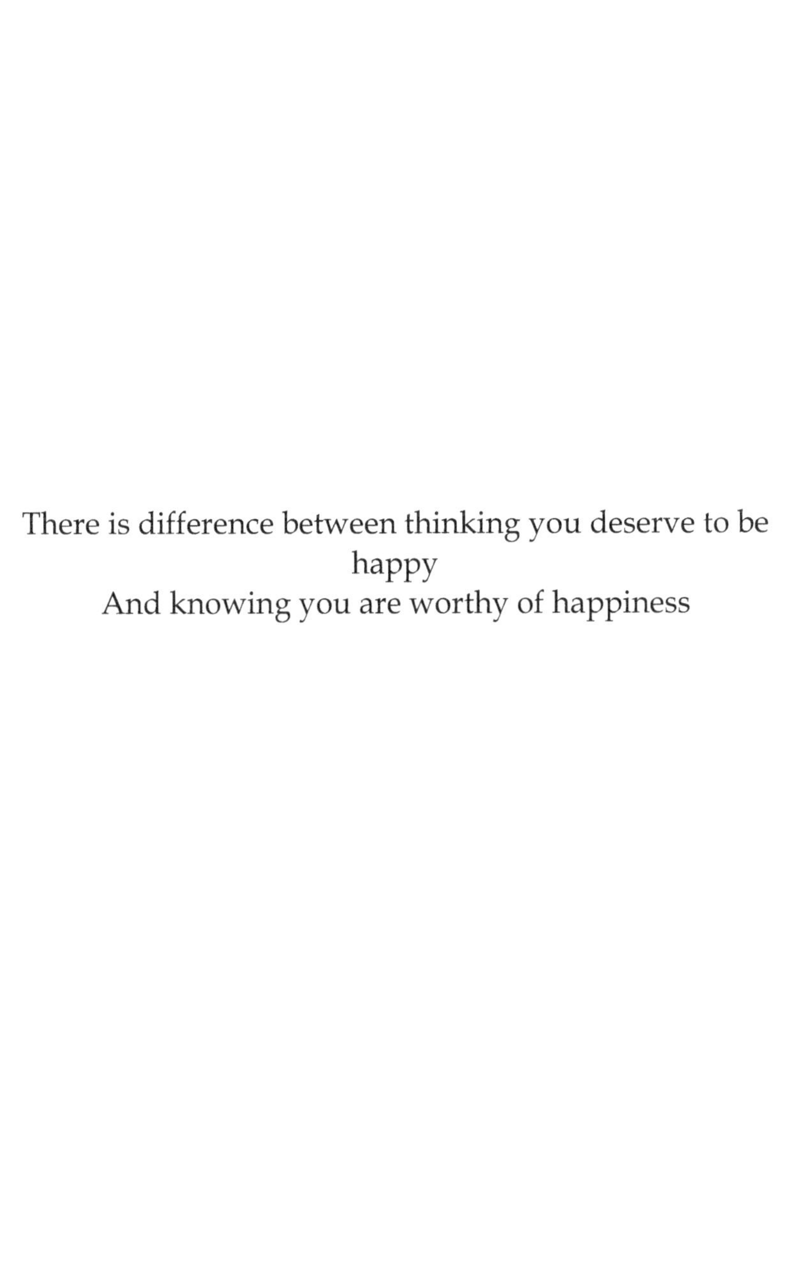

There is difference between thinking you deserve to be
happy
And knowing you are worthy of happiness

You are worthy

Chapter 11

Every day we have to test our will power.
You have to choose between getting off the couch or exercising.
Junk food or healthy food.
Binge watching TV or doing something productive.

Long term happiness takes short term sacrifices.

But please remember this, happy people have bad moments too.

I am messy. I am far from perfect.
I am not always patient, kind, and well…nice.
I am a cancer. If you don't know anything about that, that means I am moody.
I get a little road rage(y) when I am in a hurry because I do not like to be late.
I have an anxiety disorder and suffer with panic attacks.
My children are older, but sometimes I still snap at them.

None of that means I am not a happy person, it means I am human.

Happiness, true happiness, in my opinion is a way of life. Like the saying goes, "Was it really a bad day or was it a bad five minutes that you have milked all day?"

Everyone experiences bad days. But if you spend your time sulking in self-pity over minor setbacks – well you are robbing yourself of happiness. It is okay to have a bad day, it's okay to want to just sit on the couch and do nothing all day. What is not okay is for you to live there. What is not okay is to not recover from it.

So, your husband got snappy with you at dinner. Okay…. Is he in charge of your happiness?

Your boss embarrassed during a meeting with coworkers?
Alright, is he in charge of your happiness?

You see on social media some girlfriends went out, but you weren't invited.
Ouch, I get it, but who are they when it comes to your happiness?

Your children just tracked in mud from outside all over your newly cleaned floors.
Grrr…but they aren't the ones calling the shots when it comes to your happiness, right?

When these moments happen, take a breath. Go to the bathroom, have a shot of alcohol, go for a walk, or just bawl up in the floor and cry. You do you.

But then you pick yourself right back up and tell yourself, my happiness matters….and then you make it matter. Is that dirty floor worth the price of you now having a shitty day? Nope.

One thing I struggled with the most when I made the decision that my happiness mattered, was being worthy of the happiness it brought me.

I had been so unhappy for so long; I didn't really know how to handle my own happiness. Imagine the prettiest diamond ring you have ever seen, it's worth a shit ton of money and its big and just beautiful. It makes you feel so important, pretty, sexy, rich, and successful when you put it on…but the thought of wearing it in public is scary. What if you lose it? What if someone steals it? What if people laugh at it? What if people question it? Am I worthy to wear it?

That is what my happiness felt like when I first took it back. I was scared to wear it, fear that I would be laughed at, talked about, what if someone tried to steal it, what if I lost it, or am I worthy to have it?

Here is the real irony in all of that. My name is Amanda, want to know what my name means?

Worthy of love.

I had to retrain my brain that I was worthy of happiness… and love. And by doing so, I saw real life results. I became the mother that my children deserved. They got to experience their mother truly happy for the first time in their life. My son recently told me not to long ago, I am so happy to see you so happy mom, you deserve this happiness. That right there, made it all worth it.

Then I met Joshua, he is my soulmate. We started out as friends and then that friendship turned into the most secure, loving, rewarding relationship I could have ever dreamed of. When we first started dating, I struggled a lot of even being worthy of him. I had never had a man love me the way that he loves me. I had never loved a person as much as I love him. When I say he is my everything, he is just that. My everything. We are soulmates.

Learning that my happiness matters and living my life that way has done amazing things for who I am as a person. I am a better mother, girlfriend, and person. Again, I am not perfect. I am human. I just want to help you understand that your happiness matters. Be unapologetically selfish with it.

I have a sign that hangs above my bed, it says, "you belong here" that is my daily reminder to myself that I am worthy of the happiness and the life that I have.

Remember the word selfish simply means being concerned with one's own interests. Being concerned with one's interest does not mean hurting others. The idea that being selfish is wrong, bad, and immoral comes from society which makes you sacrifice for others in order to be a moral person. But why is sacrificing for others moral, while sacrificing for yourself is immoral? Can someone please explain the rational justification for that? Because to me, the short answer is there is none.

Being truly selfish, i.e., pursing your values and achieving your happiness and achieving this for 80 years requires an incredible amount of continuous, rational thought and effort. Being selfish is actually a lot of work, but the rewards are tremendous.

Is it really in a person's best interest to rob a bank, do drugs, sleep around or be a con-artist? Are any of those activities going to allow a person to live a long life AND allow them to achieve happiness and self-esteem? Why does society call those activities selfish? That is more self – destruction, yes?

To be truly happy and psychologically healthy, you must choose, pursue, achieve and enjoy values that are personally selfish. While respecting that others can do the same. Throw off the unearned guilt and the moral code that creates it.

It's time for you to put the "I" back into identity.

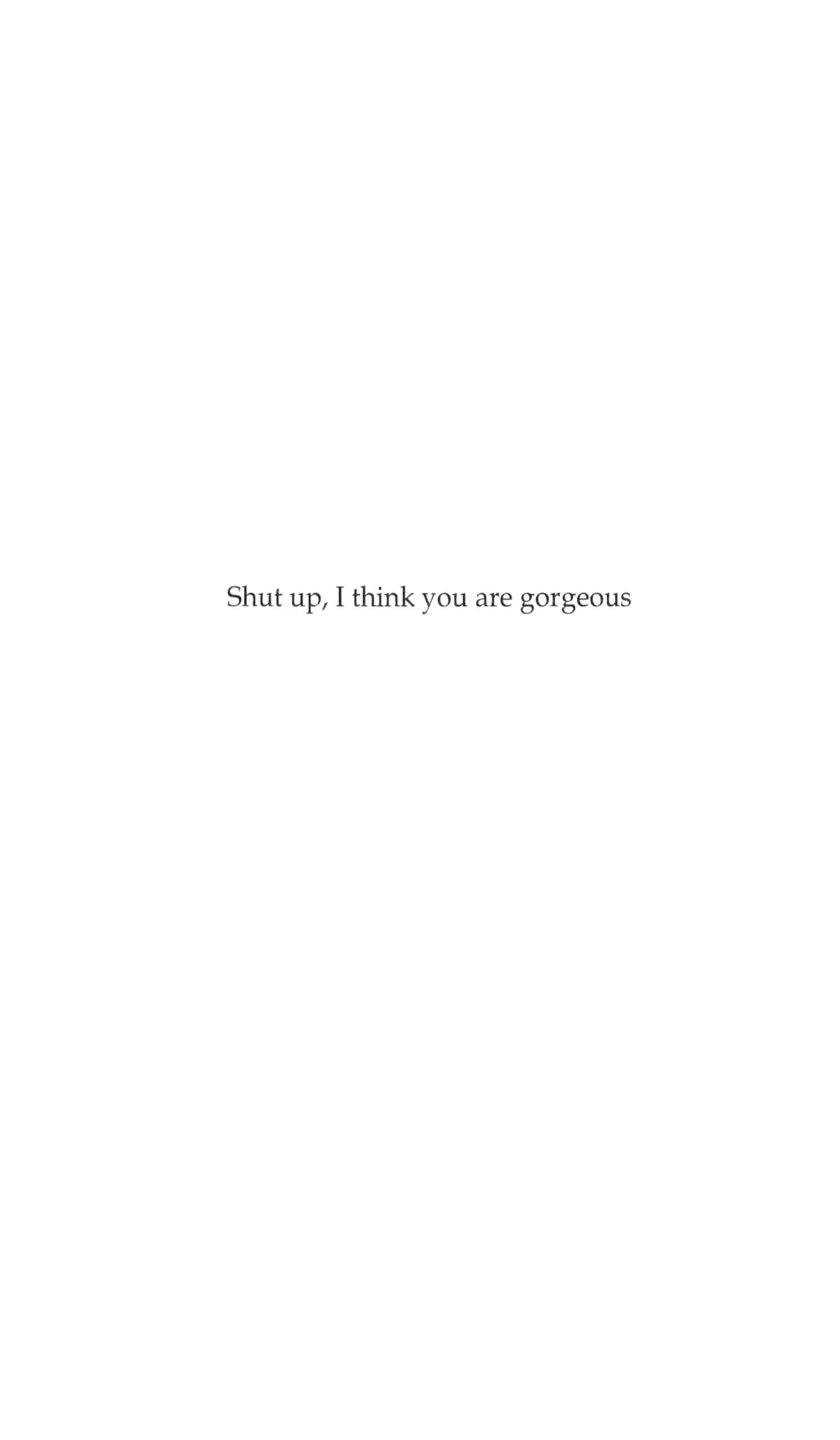

Shut up, I think you are gorgeous

Drunk girls in bathrooms

Chapter 12

Feminamity: The warm glow you get when another woman hypes you up.

No one on the planet can or will make you feel as dope as a fellow woman, three glasses of wine deep, while in the girl's bathroom.

Her compliments come across gushy, but boy are the genuine. Her opinions of your shirt, shoes, or face will make your whole night…hell week. Sometimes she might slur words of advice telling you that you would look AMAZING with shorter hair – but its never judgmental. Sometimes you exchange names with her, sometimes she is content to just let you do your thing and leave. Whatever she says to you, it will be in all caps.

The mysterious, overjoyed kindness of drunk girls has been well documented everywhere. These women mostly just exist in the small confines of a girl's bathroom walls. They are there to give you a boost, shower you with compliments, not asking for anything in return, there is no default response to the compliments, because there is no point - and then just like that. The bathroom door opens and poof they are gone.

The drunk girl in the bathroom is your confirmation that you are doing okay. You're cute, you're friendly, you are worthy of the attention – and not just in the eyes of those who know and love you. To a complete stranger.

There is no repayment that you can give the drunk girl it the bathroom, you will just walk out and go about your night. This time with a little more pep in your walk, the whole night could go to shit, but you look at it a little different now. Because you know that somewhere, in a bathroom, there is a drunk girl who thinks you are the prettiest thing she has ever seen, or well at least in the last 4 minutes.

I get it, women's role have changed. Most women no longer aspire to be a stay-at-home mom and wife. Women have careers now, building businesses from the ground up, running for presidency, leading global movements, and so much more.

However, every woman out there needs to be inspired, you are human. Stop sitting around waiting for someone else to validate your dreams and your happiness.

Be the drunk girl in the bathroom – for yourself.

No one is going to want your dreams the way that you do, and why would they? They are YOUR dreams. But by building a strong foundation in yourself, when life isn't all rainbows and unicorns you get yourself through it.

I want you to think about everything you have gone through, and all that you have accomplished. By acknowledging the challenges that you have made it through, you are going to build up trust with yourself that you can do anything. Your own beliefs have all the power to change your life. If you believe that you can't and you won't, then changes are you won't.

But if you tell yourself that you can, and you truly believe that. You can.

The belief you have in yourself has everything to do with how you see yourself in the world. If you believe you are stuck and you have no power to change whatever is making you unhappy, then you will remain a victim in your life. I want you to start believing that you an endlessly evolve and infinitely change.

The only person stopping you from your happiness is you. Not your spouse, not your children, not your job, not your parents, not even society. It's you.

I used to be totally insecure, I had zero confidence in myself as Amanda. I depended on others to validate my aspirations, and guess what, they didn't. Then I was embarrassed, I gave up trying, and I lost myself.

Then one day, I became the drunk girl in the bathroom. For myself. I hyped myself up. I told myself I was cute. I told myself I liked my hair. I told myself how freaking awesome I was. I became my cheerleader.

The day you realize your happiness matters is the day that you will become the drunk girl in the bathroom, for yourself…and for others, because never forget that happiness is scientifically proven to spread. So, if you are standing next to someone in the frozen food section and you like their shoes, say it. Make them feel awesome. Boost them up. Our children are watching, they cannot witness the lovefest in the bathrooms, but they can see how we are treating people, and that is how they learn to treat people. So, in my opinion, throwing out compliments like a drunk girl in the bathroom isn't just spreading sunshine to those around us, its sowing the seeds of a brighter future as well.

By the way, I love your top and you have an excellent taste in reading material.

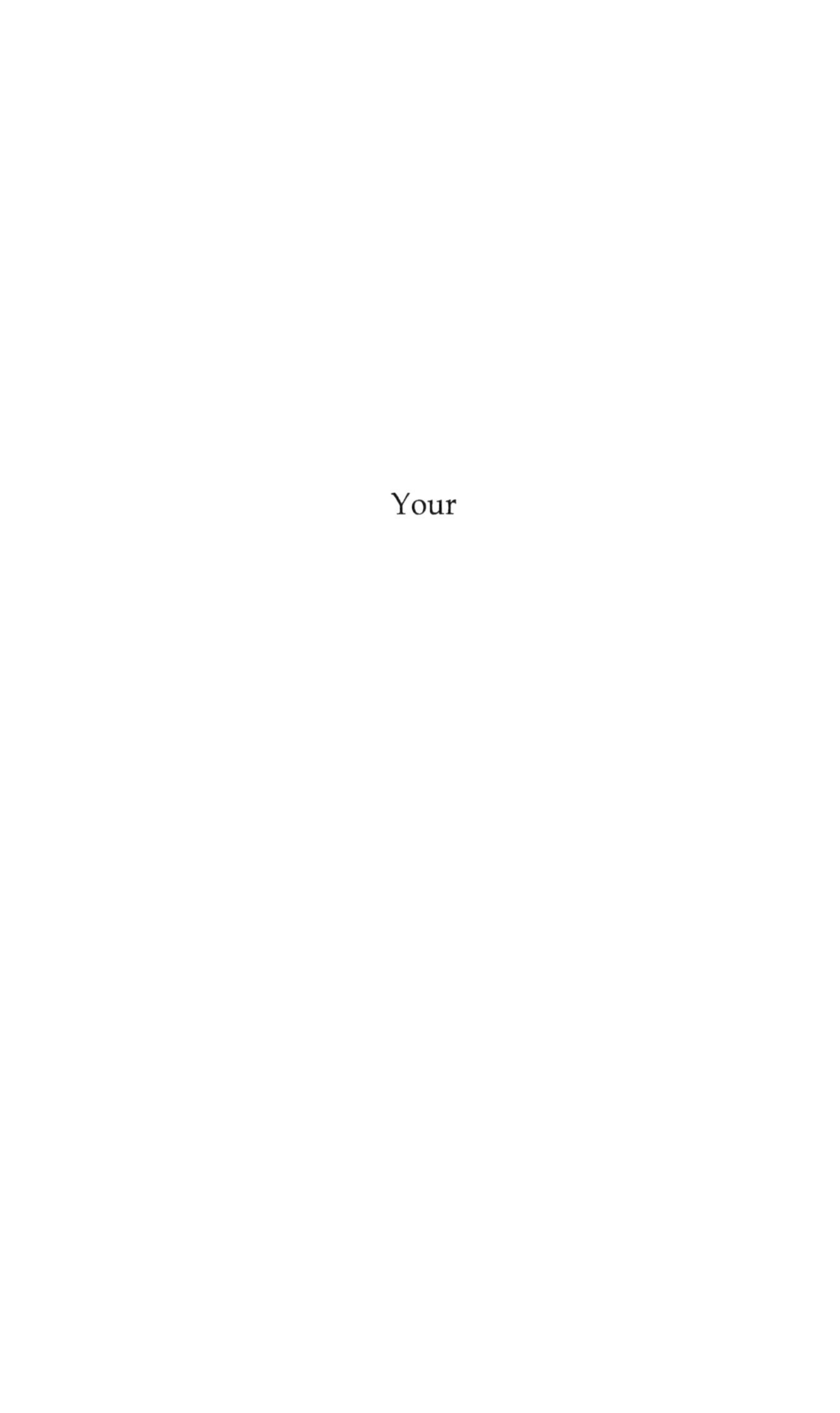

Your

Happiness

Matters

The Big Question

Chapter 13

So, I have one last question for you. One that I am
going to leave you with.
One that my therapist asked me.
One that truly took the rose color off my glasses more
than anything else.

I will never forget this day and my hope is its impactful
for you. But I am warning you, it is not going to be
comfortable.

I was in therapy, doing what you do while in session,
talking, rambling, venting, crying, etc … when I was
done, I told my therapist, "I just don't know what to
do"

She looked at me and confidently said, I want you to
imagine that I am your daughter, but your daughter is
the same age as you right now, and I just told you, as
your daughter, everything you just told me. What
would you tell me to do? Then after some silence, she
said that's right, you know what to do. Now tell me
why you want better for your daughter than you do for
yourself?

So, I am asking you that same question.

No need to answer, I know the answer and girl, oh girl.
I am so incredibly proud of you and I am here in
Oklahoma being the biggest hype girl for you right
now!!!!

BE YOU
DO YOU
FOR YOU

YOUR HAPPINESS MATTERS
NOW GO BE SELFISH WITH IT

Xoxo
Amanda

Reasons you should be selfish with your happiness

1. Being selfish in some areas can allow you to be more generous in others
2. You'll have more time for the things that you love
3. You can stop blaming others for your problems
4. You will be physically and emotionally healthier
5. You will feel more balanced
6. Thinking about yourself prevents autopilot
7. You learn to be your own advocate
8. You will inspire others
9. You will gain self confidence
10. Valuing yourself
11. You matter.

But what will the neighbors think?

Your happiness matters

- But what about the kids?
    - i. *Your happiness matters*
- But what about the house?
    - i. *Your happiness matters*
- But my family doesn't get divorces
    - i. *Your happiness matters*
- But my kid just fell down – and there is blood
    - i. Well, you should probably check on them
- But they have been planning this for a long time
    - i. *Your happiness matters*
- But I am supposed to bring cookies
    - i. *Your happiness matters*
- But the holidays are coming up
    - i. *Your happiness matters*
- But I am afraid of being alone
    - i. *Your happiness matters*
- But divorce is expensive
    - i. *Your happiness matters*
- But my boss is nice some days
    - i. *Your happiness matters*
- But I don't like confrontation
    - i. *Your happiness matters*
- But I am a stay-at-home mom
    - i. *Your happiness matters*

- But they need my help
    - *i.   Your happiness matters*
- But I don't have any skills
    - *i.   Your happiness matters*
- But I don't have any savings
    - *i.   Your happiness matters*
- But we just bought a new car
    - *i.   Your happiness matters*
- But I didn't go to college
    - *i.   Your happiness matters*
- But I don't have time
    - *i.   Your happiness matters*
- But it might get better
    - *i.   Your happiness matters*
- But quitting looks bad
    - *i.   Your happiness matters*
- But what will my friends say
    - *i.   Your happiness matters*
- But I will lose my company car
    - *i.   Your happiness matters*
- But we are going on vacation soon
    - i.   Where ya going? Is it the beach?
- But I will lose my health insurance
    - *i.   Your happiness matters*
- But what will my church think of me
    - *i.   Your happiness matters*
- But I don't have any family here
    - *i.   Your happiness matters*
- But I would have to start working
    - *i.   Your happiness matters*
- But the kids would have to go to daycare
    - *i.   Your happiness matters*

- But I have known him since high school
    - *i. Your happiness matters*
- But I am ____ years old
    - *i. Your happiness matters*
- But I might let some people down
    - *i. Your happiness matters*
- But there is a big report due next week
    - *i. Your happiness matters*
- Our anniversary is coming up
    - *i. Your happiness matters*
- But I need to get gas
    - *i. I bet I do to, I hate pumping gas*
- But people are going to talk
    - *i. Your happiness matters*
- But he is busy
    - *i. Your happiness matters*
- But I am just an emotional person
    - *i. Your happiness matters*
- But he just made a mistake
    - *i. Your happiness matters*
- But I bet I can change him
    - *i. Your happiness matters*
- But I might lose some friends
    - *i. Your happiness matters*

Listen, we can all come up with a million different reasons why you cannot move from the position you're in right now. But girl, I am here to tell you.

Your Happiness Matters

www.ingramcontent.com/pod-product-compliance
Lightning Source LLC
Chambersburg PA
CBHW071927120726

48001CB00005B/1901